BY MAYA ANGELOU

LETTER TO MY DAUGHTER

LETTER TO
MY DAUGHTER

Maya Angelou

RANDOM HOUSE
TRADE PAPERBACKS
NEW YORK

Published in the United States by Random House Trade Paperbacks,
an imprint of The Random House Publishing Group,
a division of Random House, Inc., New York.

RANDOM HOUSE TRADE PAPERBACKS and colophon are
trademarks of Random House, Inc.

Originally published in hardcover in the United States by Random House,
an imprint of The Random House Publishing Group,
a division of Random House, Inc., in 2008.

Grateful acknowledgement is made to the following for permission
to reprint previously published material:

Mari Evans: Excerpt from "I Am a Black Woman" from *I Am a Black Woman*
by Mari Evans (New York: William Morrow, 1970). Reprinted by
permission of Mari Evans.

Alfred A. Knopf, a division of Random House, Inc. and Harold Ober Associates:
"I, Too" and "Dream Variations" from *The Collected Poems of Langston Hughes*
by Langston Hughes, edited by Arnold Rampersad with David Russell,
associate editor, copyright © 1994 by the Estate of Langston Hughes.
Rights in the United Kingdom are controlled by Harold Ober Associates.
Reprinted by permission of Alfred A. Knopf, a division of Random
House, Inc., and Harold Ober Associates Incorporated.

Melvin B. Tolson, Jr. c/o The Permissions Company: Excerpt from "Dark Symphony"
from *Rendezvous with America* (New York: Dodd, Mead, 1944). Originally
published in *Atlantic Monthly* (September 1941), copyright © 1941, 1944 by
Melvin B. Tolson and copyright renewed 1969, 1972 by Ruth S. Tolson.
Reprinted by permission of Melvin B. Tolson, Jr. c/o The Permissions
Company, www.permissionscompany.com.

LIBRARY OF CONGRESS CATALOGING-IN-PUBLICATION DATA

Angelou, Maya.
Letter to my daughter / Maya Angelou.
p.   cm.
ISBN 978-0-8129-8003-5 (alk. paper)
1. Angelou, Maya.   2. Authors, American—Homes and haunts—New York
(State)—New York.   3. African American authors—Biography.
4. Authors, American—20th century—Biography.   I. Title.
PS3551.N464Z468 2008
818'.5409—dc22   2008028843
[B]

Printed in the United States of America

www.atrandom.com

28 30 32 34 35 33 31 29

Book design by Carole Lowenstein

My thanks to some women who mothered me
through dark and bright days,

Annie Henderson
Vivian Baxter
Frances Williams
Berdis Baldwin
Amisher Glenn

My thanks to one woman who allows me
to be a daughter to her, even today,

Dr. Dorothy Height

My thanks to women not born to me but who allow me
to mother them,

Oprah Winfrey
Rosa Johnson Butler
Lydia Stuckey
Gayle B. King
Valerie Simpson
Stephenie Floyd Johnson
Dinky Weber
Brenda Crisp
Bettie Clay
Araba Bernasko
Frances Berry
Patricia Casey

CONTENTS

CONTENTS

LETTER TO MY DAUGHTER

Dear Daughter,

This letter has taken an extraordinary time getting itself together. I have all along known that I wanted to tell you directly of some lessons I have learned and under what conditions I have learned them.

My life has been long, and believing that life loves the liver of it, I have dared to try many things, sometimes trembling, but daring, still. I have only included here events and lessons which I have found useful. I have not told how I have used the solutions, knowing that you are intelligent and creative and resourceful and you will use them as you see fit.

You will find in this book accounts of growing up, unexpected emergencies, a few poems, some light stories to make you laugh and some to make you meditate.

There have been people in my life who meant me well, taught me valuable lessons, and others who have meant me ill and, have given me ample notification that my world is not meant to be all peaches and cream.

I have made many mistakes and no doubt will make more before I die. When I have seen pain, when I have found that my ineptness has caused displeasure, I have learned to accept my responsibility and to forgive myself first, then to apologize to anyone injured by my misreckoning. Since I cannot un-live history, and repentance is all I can offer God, I have hopes that my sincere apologies were accepted.

You may not control all the events that happen to you, but you can decide not to be reduced by them. Try to be a rainbow in someone's cloud. Do not complain. Make every effort to change things you do not like. If you cannot make a change, change the way you have been thinking. You might find a new solution.

Never whine. Whining lets a brute know that a victim is in the neighborhood.

Be certain that you do not die without having done something wonderful for humanity.

I gave birth to one child, a son, but I have thousands of daughters. You are Black and White, Jewish and Muslim, Asian, Spanish-speaking, Native American and Aleut. You are fat and thin and pretty and plain, gay and straight, educated and unlettered, and I am speaking to you all. Here is my offering to you.

LETTER TO MY DAUGHTER

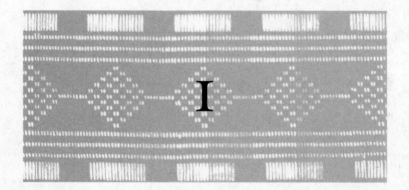

Home

I was born in St. Louis, Missouri, but from the age of three I grew up in Stamps, Arkansas, with my paternal grandmother, Annie Henderson, and my father's brother, Uncle Willie, and my only sibling, my brother Bailey.

At thirteen I joined my mother in San Francisco. Later I studied in New York City. Throughout the years I have lived in Paris, Cairo, West Africa, and all over the United States.

Those are facts, but facts, to a child, are merely words to memorize, "My name is Johnny Thomas. My address is 220 Center Street." All facts, which have little to do with the child's truth.

My real growing up world, in Stamps, was a continual struggle against a condition of surrender. Surrender first to the grown-up human beings who I saw every day, all black and all very, very large. Then submission to the idea that black people were inferior to white people, who I saw rarely.

Without knowing why exactly, I did not believe that I was

inferior to anyone except maybe my brother. I knew I was smart, but I also knew that Bailey was smarter, maybe because he reminded me often and even suggested that maybe he was the smartest person in the world. He came to that decision when he was nine years old.

The South, in general, and Stamps, Arkansas, in particular had had hundreds of years' experience in demoting even large adult blacks to psychological dwarfs. Poor white children had the license to address lauded and older blacks by their first names or by any names they could create.

Thomas Wolfe warned in the title of America's great novel that "you can't go home again." I enjoyed the book but I never agreed with the title. I believe that one can never leave home. I believe that one carries the shadows, the dreams, the fears and dragons of home under one's skin, at the extreme corners of one's eyes and possibly in the gristle of the earlobe.

Home is that youthful region where a child is the only real living inhabitant. Parents, siblings, and neighbors are mysterious apparitions who come, go, and do strange unfathomable things in and around the child, the region's only enfranchised citizen.

Geography, as such, has little meaning to the child observer. If one grows up in the Southwest, the desert and open skies are natural. New York, with the elevators and subway rumble and millions of people, and Southeast Florida, with its palm trees and sun and beaches, are to the children of those regions the way the outer world is, has been, and will always be. Since the child cannot control that environment, she has to find her own place, a region where only she lives and no one else can enter.

I am convinced that most people do not grow up. We find

parking spaces and honor our credit cards. We marry and dare to have children and call that growing up. I think what we do is mostly grow old. We carry accumulation of years in our bodies and on our faces, but generally our real selves, the children inside, are still innocent and shy as magnolias.

We may act sophisticated and worldly but I believe we feel safest when we go inside ourselves and find home, a place where we belong and maybe the only place we really do.

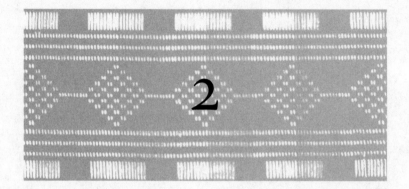

2

Philanthropy

To write about giving to a person who is naturally generous reminds me of a preacher passionately preaching to the already committed choir. I am encouraged to write on because I remember that from time to time, the choir does need to be uplifted and thanked for its commitment. Those voices need to be encouraged to sing again and again, with even more emotion.

Each single American giver keeps alive the American Cancer Society, the Red Cross, Salvation Army, Goodwill, Sickle Cell Anemia, American Jewish Society, NAACP, and the Urban League. The list continues to include church foundations, synagogue programs, Muslim Temple associations, Buddhist shrines, groups, officials, and city and social clubs. However, the largest sums of money come from philanthropists.

The word philanthropy was taken from the two Greek words, *philo*—lover of; and *anthro*—mankind. So, philanthropists are lovers of humanity. They build imposing edifices for people to work in and to play in. They give huge sums of money to support organizations which offer better health and education to the society. They are the principal patrons of the arts.

The mention of philanthropy elicits smiles, followed by the sensation of receiving unexpected good fortune from a generous but faceless source.

There are those who would like to see themselves as philanthropists. Philanthropists often are represented by committees and delegations. They are disconnected from the recipients of their generosity. I am not a member of that gathering. Rather I like to think of myself as charitable. The charitable say in effect, "I seem to have more than I need and you seem to have less than you need. I would like to share my excess with you." Fine, if my excess is tangible, money or goods, and fine if not, for I learned that to be charitable with gestures and words can bring enormous joy and repair injured feelings.

My paternal grandmother, who raised me, had a remarkable influence on how I saw the world and how I reckoned my place in it. She was the picture of dignity. She spoke softly and walked slowly, with her hands behind her back, fingers laced together. I imitated her so successfully that neighbors called me her shadow.

"Sister Henderson, I see you got your shadow with you again."

Grandmother would look at me and smile. "Well, I guess you're right. If I stop, she stops. If I go, she goes."

When I was thirteen, my grandmother took me back to California to join my mother, and she returned immediately to Arkansas. The California house was a world away from that little home in which I grew up in Arkansas. My mother wore her straight hair in a severe stylish bob. My grandmother didn't believe in hot-curling women's hair, so I had grown up with a braided natural. Grandmother turned our radio on to listen to the news, religious music, *Gang Busters,* and *The Lone Ranger.* In California my mother wore lipstick and rouge and played loud blues and jazz music on a record player. Her house was full of people who laughed a lot and talked loudly. I definitely did not belong. I walked around in that worldly atmosphere with my hands clasped behind my back, my hair pulled back in a tight braid, humming a Christian song.

My mother watched me for about two weeks. Then we had what was to become familiar as "a sit-down talk-to."

She said, "Maya, you disapprove of me because I am not like your grandmother. That's true. I am not. But I am your mother and I am working some part of my anatomy off to buy you good clothes and give you well-prepared food and keep this roof over your head. When you go to school, the teacher will smile at you and you will smile back. Other students you don't even know will smile and you will smile. But on the other hand, I am your mother. I tell you what I want you to do. If you can force one smile on your face for strangers, do it for me. I promise you I will appreciate it."

She put her hand on my cheek and smiled. "Come on, baby, smile for Mother. Come on."

She made a funny face, and against my wishes I smiled. She kissed me on the lips and started to cry.

"That's the first time I have seen you smile. It is a beautiful smile. Mother's beautiful daughter can smile."

I had never been called beautiful and no one in my memory had ever called me daughter.

That day, I learned that I could be a giver by simply bringing a smile to another person. The ensuing years have taught me that a kind word, a vote of support is a charitable gift. I can move over and make another place for someone. I can turn my music up if it pleases, or down if it is annoying.

I may never be known as a philanthropist, but I certainly am a lover of mankind, and I will give freely of my resources.

I am happy to describe myself as charitable.

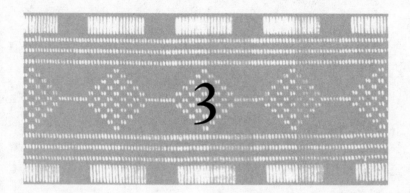

3

Revelations

It had to be the days of Revelations. The days John the revelator prophesied. The earth shuddered as trains thundered up and down in its black belly. Private cars, taxis, buses, surface trains, trucks, delivery vans, cement mixers, delivery carts, bicycles, and skates occupied the air with honks, toots, roars, thuds, screams, and whistles, until the very air seemed thick and lumpy like bad gravy.

People from everywhere, speaking every known language, had come to town to watch the end and the beginning of the world.

I wanted to forget about the enormity of the day, so I went to the Fillmore Street 5 & Dime store. It was an acre-wide shop where dreams hung on plastic stands. I had walked up and down its aisles a thousand times over. I knew its seductive magic. From the nylon slips with cardboard tits to the cosmetic counter where lipsticks and nail polish were pink and red and green and blue fruits fallen from a rainbow tree.

That was the city, when I was sixteen and brand new like daybreak.

The day was so important I could hardly breathe.

A boy who lived up the street from me had been asking me to be intimate with him. I had refused for months. He was not my boyfriend. We were not even dating.

It was during that time that I noticed my body's betrayal. My voice became deep and husky, and my naked image in the mirror gave no intimations that it would ever become feminine and curvy.

I was already six feet tall and had no breasts. I thought maybe if I had sex my recalcitrant body would grow up and behave as it was supposed to behave.

That morning the boy had telephoned and I told him yes. He gave me an address and said he would meet me there at 8:00 o'clock. I said yes.

A friend had lent him his apartment. From the moment I saw him at the door I knew I had made the wrong choice. There were no endearments spoken, no warm caresses shared.

He showed me to a bedroom, where we both undressed. The fumbling engagement lasted fifteen minutes, and I had my clothes on and was at the front door.

I don't remember if we said goodbye.

I do remember walking down the street, wondering was that all there was and how much I wanted a long soaking bath. I did get the bath and that was not all there was.

Nine months later, I had a beautiful baby boy. The birth of my son caused me to develop enough courage to invent my life.

I learned to love my son without wanting to possess him and I learned how to teach him to teach himself.

Today, over forty years later, when I look at him and see the wonderful man he has become, the loving husband and father, the good poet and fine novelist, the responsible citizen and the world's greatest son, I thank the Creator that he was given to me. The Revelation is that day, so long ago, was the greatest day of my life—*Hallelujah!*

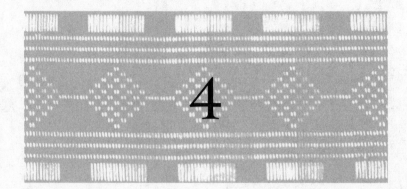

Giving Birth

My brother, Bailey, told me to keep my pregnancy a secret from my mother. He said she would take me out of school. I was very close to graduating. Bailey said I had to have a high school diploma before mother returned to San Francisco from the nightclub she and her husband owned in Nome, Alaska.

I received my diploma on VJ Day, which was also my stepfather's birthday. He had patted me on the shoulder that morning and said, "You are growing up and you are becoming a fine young woman." I thought to myself: I should, I am eight months and one week pregnant.

After a salutary dinner celebrating his birthday, my graduation, and a national victory, I left a note on his pillow saying, "Dad, I am sorry to bring disgrace to the family, but I have to tell you that I am pregnant." I didn't sleep that night.

I heard my dad go to his room about 3:00 A.M. When he didn't knock on my door immediately, I puzzled over whether he had seen and read the note. There would be no sleep for me that night.

At 8:30 in the morning he spoke at my door.

He said, "Baby, come down and have coffee with me, by the way—I got your note."

The sound of him walking away was not nearly as loud as the sound of my heart racing. Downstairs at the table he said, "I'm going to call your mother. How far along are you?"

I said, "I have three weeks."

He smiled. "I'm sure your mother will be here today."

Nervous and frightened are not words which even barely describe how I was feeling.

Before nightfall my pretty little mother walked into the house. She gave me a kiss, then looked at me. "You're more than any three weeks pregnant."

I said, "No, ma'am, I'm eight months and one week pregnant."

She asked, "Who is the boy?" I told her.

She asked, "Do you love him?"

I said, "No."

"Does he love you?"

I said, "No, he's the only person with whom I had sex and we were together only one time."

My mother said, "There is no reason to ruin three lives; our family is going to have a wonderful baby."

She was a registered nurse, so when I began labor she shaved me, powdered me and took me to the hospital. The doctor had not arrived. Mother introduced herself to the nurses and said that as a nurse herself, she was going to help with the delivery.

She crawled up on the delivery table with me and had me

bend my legs. She put her shoulder against my knee and told me dirty stories. When the pains came she told me the punch line of the stories, and as I laughed she told me, "Bear down."

When the baby started coming, my little mother jumped off the table, and seeing him emerge she shouted, "Here he comes and he has black hair." I wondered what color she thought he might have.

When the baby was delivered, my mother caught him. She and the other nurses cleaned him and wrapped him in a blanket, and she brought him to me. "Here, my baby, here's your beautiful baby."

My dad said that when she returned home she was so tired she looked as if she had given birth to quintuplets.

She was so proud of her grandson and proud of me. I never had to spend one minute regretting giving birth to a child who had a devoted family led by a fearless, doting, and glorious grandmother. So I became proud of myself.

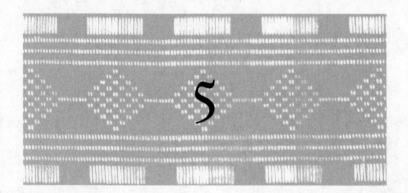

5

Accident, Coincident,
or Answered Prayer

His name was Mark. He was tall and well built. If good looks were horses, he could seat the entire Royal Canadian Mounties. Mark was inspired by Joe Louis. He left Texas, where he was born and found work in Detroit. There he intended to make enough money to find a trainer and become a professional boxer.

A machine in the automotive plant cut three fingers off his right hand and his dream perished. When I met him he told me the story and explained why he was known as Two Finger Mark. He did not show any rancor about his dreams deferred. He spoke softly to me and often paid for a babysitter so that I could visit him in his rented room. He was an ideal suitor. He was a lover with a slow hand. I felt absolutely safe and secure.

After a few months of his tender attention, he picked me

up one night from my job and said he was taking me out to Half Moon Bay.

He parked on a cliff, and through the windows I saw the moonlight silver on the rippling water.

I got out of the car, and when he said, "Come over here," I went immediately.

He said, "You've got another man, and you've been lying to me." I started to laugh. I was still laughing when he hit me. Before I could breathe he had hit me in the face with both fists. I did see stars before I fell.

When I came to, he had removed most of my clothes and leaned me against an outcropping of rock. He had a large wooden slat in his hand and he was crying.

"I treated you so well, you lousy cheating, low-down woman." I tried to walk to him but my legs would not support me. Then he hit the back of my head with the board. I passed out. Each time I came to, I saw that he continued to cry and to beat me and I continued to pass out.

I must depend on hearsay for the events of the next few hours.

Mark put me into the backseat of his car and drove to the African American area in San Francisco. He parked in front of Betty Lou's Chicken Shack and called some hangers-around and showed me to them.

"This is what you do with a lying cheating broad."

They recognized me and returned to the restaurant. They told Miss Betty Lou that Mark had Vivian's daughter in the back of his car and she looks dead.

Miss Betty Lou and my mother were close friends. Miss Betty Lou phoned my mother.

No one knew where he lived or worked or even his last name.

Because of the pool halls and gambling clubs my mother owned, and the police contacts Miss Betty Lou had, they expected to find Mark quickly.

My mother was close with the leading bail bondsman in San Francisco. So she telephoned him. Boyd Pucinelli had no Mark or Two Finger Mark in his files.

He promised Vivian he would continue to search.

I awakened to find I was in a bed and I was sore all over. It hurt to breathe, to try to speak. Mark said that was because I had broken ribs. My lips had been speared by my teeth.

He started to cry, saying he loved me. He brought a double-edged razor blade and put it to his throat.

"I'm not worth living, I should kill myself."

I had no voice to discourage him. He quickly put the razor blade on my throat.

"I can't leave you here for some other Negro to have you." Speaking was impossible and breathing was painful.

Suddenly he changed his mind.

"You haven't eaten for three days. I've got to get you some juice. Do you like pineapple juice and orange juice? Just nod your head."

I didn't know what to do. What would send him off?

"I'm going to the corner store to get you some juice. I'm sorry that I hurt you. When I come back, I'm going to nurse you back to health, full health, I promise."

I watched him leave.

Only then did I recognize that I was in his room, where I had been often. I knew his landlady lived on the same floor, and I thought that if I could get her attention, she would help me. I inhaled as much air as I could take and tried to shout, but no sounds would come. The pain of trying to sit up was so extreme that I tried only once.

I knew where he had put the razor blade. If I could get it, at least I could take my own life and he would be prevented from gloating that he killed me.

I began to pray.

I passed in and out of prayer, in and out of consciousness, and then I heard shouting down the hall. I heard my mother's voice.

"Break it down. Break the son of a bitch down. My baby's in there." Wood groaned then splintered and the door gave way and my little mother walked through the opening. She saw me and fainted. Later she told me that was the only time in her life she had done so.

The sight of my face swollen twice its size and my teeth stuck into my lips was more than she could stand. So she fell. Three huge men followed her into the room. Two picked her up and she came to in their arms groggily. They brought her to my bed.

"Baby, baby, I'm so sorry." Each time she touched me, I flinched. "Call for an ambulance. I'll kill the bastard. I'm sorry."

She felt guilty like all mothers who blamed themselves when terrible events happen to their children.

I could not speak or even touch her but I have never loved her more than at that moment in that suffocating stinking room.

She patted my face and stroked my arm.

"Baby, somebody's prayers were answered. No one knew how to find Mark, even Boyd Pucinelli. But Mark went to a mom-and-pop store to buy juice and two kids robbed a to-bacco vendor's truck." She continued telling her story.

"When a police car turned the corner, the young boys threw the cartons of cigarettes in Mark's car. When he tried to get into his car, the police arrested him. They didn't believe his cries of innocence, so they took him to jail. He used his one phone call to telephone Boyd Pucinelli. Boyd answered the phone."

Mark said, "My name is Mark Jones, I live on Oak Street. I don't have money with me now, but my landlady is holding a lot of my money. If you call her she will come down and bring whatever you charge."

Boyd asked, "What is your street name?" Mark said, "I'm called Two Finger Mark." Boyd hung up and called my mother, giving her Mark's address. He asked if she would call the police. She said, "No I'm going to my pool hall and get some rough-necks then I'm going to get my daughter."

She said that when she arrived at Mark's house, his land-lady said she didn't know any Mark and anyway he hadn't been home for days.

Mother said maybe not, but she was looking for her daugh-ter and she was in that house in Mark's room. Mother asked for Mark's room. The landlady said he keeps his door locked. My mother said, "It will open today." The landlady threatened to call the police, and my mother said, "You can call for the cook, call for the baker, you may as well call for the undertaker."

When the woman pointed out Mark's room, my mother said to her helpers, "Break it down, break the son of a bitch down."

In the hospital room I thought about the two young crim-inals who threw stolen cigarette cartons into a stranger's car.

When he was arrested he called Boyd Pucinelli, who called my mother, who gathered three of the most daring men from her pool hall.

They broke down the door of the room where I was being held. My life was saved. Was that event incident, coincident, accident, or answered prayer?

I believe my prayers were answered.

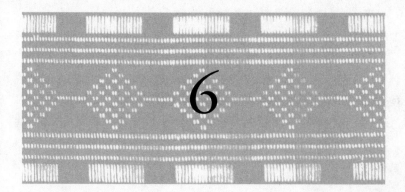

To Tell the Truth

My mother, Vivian Baxter, warned me often not to believe that people really want the truth when they ask, "How are you?" She said that question was asked around the world in thousands of languages and most people knew that it is simply a conversation starter. No one really expects to be answered, or even wants to know "Well my knees feel like they are broken, and my back hurts so bad I could fall down and cry." A response like that would be a conversation stopper. It would end before it could begin. So, we all say, "Fine, thank you, and you?"

I believe in that way we learn to give and receive social lies. We look at friends who have lost dangerous amounts of weight or who have added ungainly pounds and we say, "You're looking good." Everybody knows the statement is a blatant lie but, we all swallow the untruth in part to keep the peace and in part because we do not wish to deal with the truth. I wish we could stop the little lies. I don't mean that one has to be brutally frank. I don't believe that we should be brutal about anything, however, it is wonderfully liberating to be honest. One does not have to tell all that one knows, but we should be careful what we do say is the truth.

Let us bravely say to our young women, "That raggedy hairstyle may be trendy, but it is also unattractive. It is not doing anything for you." And let us say to our young men, "Your shirttail hanging out from under your jacket does not make you look cool, it just makes you look unkempt and uncared for." Some Hollywood fashion police decided recently that appearing in wrinkled clothes with half-shaven faces was sexy because it made men look as if they had just arisen. The fashionistas were both right and wrong. The disheveled look does make the person appear to have just gotten out of bed, but they are also wrong because that look is not sexy, it is just tacky.

The nose, nipple, and tongue rings are the possession of the very young who are experimenting. While I don't like them, they don't bother me much because I know that most of the youth will grow older and will join the social sets in which they work and live. The rings will be discarded and the young people will pray that the holes heal over so that they will not have to explain to their own teenagers why the holes were put there in the first place.

Let's tell the truth to the people. When people ask, "How are you," have the nerve sometimes to answer truthfully. You must know however, that people will start avoiding you because they too have knees that pain them and heads which hurt and they don't want to know about yours. But think of it this way, if people avoid you, you will have more time to meditate and do fine research on a cure for whatever truly afflicts you.

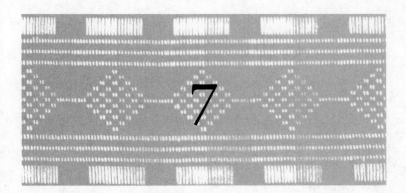

Vulgarity

Some entertainers have tried to make art of their coarseness, but in their public crudeness they have merely revealed their own vast senses of personal inferiority. When they heap mud upon themselves and allow their tongues to wag with vulgarity, they expose their belief that they are not worth loving and in fact are unlovable. When we as audience indulge them in their profanity, we are like the audience at the Roman Colosseum being thrilled as the raging lions kill the unarmed Christians. We not only participate in the humiliation of the entertainers, but we are brought low by sharing in the obscenity.

We need to have the courage to say obesity is not funny and vulgarity is not amusing. Insolent children and submissive parents are not the characters we want to admire and emulate. Flippancy and sarcasm are not the qualities which we need to include in our daily conversations.

If the emperor is standing in my living room stripped to the buff, nothing should prevent me from saying that since he has no clothes on, he is not ready for public congress. At any rate, not lounging on my sofa and munching on my trail mix.

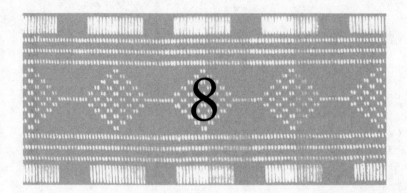

8

Violence

When our learned teachers and erudite professors misjudge
their research and misspeak their findings, it might be gracious
to turn away quietly and, whispering adieu, leave their company and, to quote Shakespeare in *Julius Caesar,* "look on injustice with a serene countenance."

Upon certain subjects I am able to hold my tongue and
hope that time will right wrongs. But there is one matter which
calls me to adversarial attention. Too many sociologists and social scientists have declared that the act of rape is not a sexual
act at all but rather a need, a need to feel powerful. They fur-
ther explain that the rapist is most often the victim of another
who was seeking power, a person who himself was a victim,
et cetera ad nauseam. Possibly some small percentage of the
motivation which impels a rapist on his savage rampage stems
from the hunger for domination, but I am certain that the violator's stimulus is (devastatingly) sexual.

The sounds of the premeditated rape, the grunts and gurgles, the sputtering and spitting, which commences when the predator spots and then targets the victim, is sexual. The stalking becomes, in the rapist's mind, a private courtship, where the courted is unaware of her suitor, but the suitor is obsessed with the object of his desire. He follows, observes, and is the excited protagonist in his sexual drama.

The impulsive rape is no less sexual, merely less extenuated. The violator who stumbles upon his unprotected victim is sexually agitated by surprise. He experiences the same vulgar rush as the flasher, save that his pleasure is not satisfied with brief shock, he has a surge and moves on to the deeper, more terrifying, invasion.

I am concerned that the pundits, who wish to shape our thinking and, subsequently, our laws, too often make rape an acceptable and even explainable social occurrence. If rape is merely about the possession of power, the search for and the exercising of power, we must simply understand and even forgive the natural human action of sex in the extreme. I believe that profanity directed at the victim of rape or equally lugubrious declarations of eternal love dribbled into the terrified victim's ear, have less to do with power than with sexual indulgence.

We must call the ravening act of rape, the bloody, heart-stopping, breath-snatching, bone-crushing act of violence, which it is. The threat makes some female and male victims unable to open their front doors, unable to venture into streets in which they grew up, unable to trust other human beings and even themselves. Let us call it a violent unredeemable sexual act.

I remember a reaction by a male friend, when a macho fellow told him that miniskirts were driving him to thoughts of rape.

My friend asked, if a woman wore a micro mini and no underpants would the would-be rapist be able to control himself? He added, "What if her big brothers were standing by holding baseball bats?"

I am concerned that accepting the power theory trivializes and diminishes the raw ugliness of the act, and dulls the razor's cruel edge of violation.

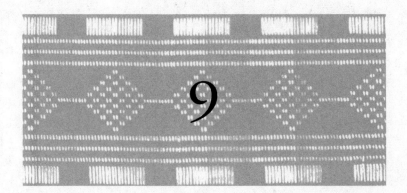

9

Mother's Long View

Independence is a heady draft, and if you drink it in your youth it can have the same effect on the brain as young wine. It does not matter that its taste is not very appealing, it is addictive and with each drink the consumer wants more.

When I was twenty-two and living in San Francisco, I had a five-year-old son, two jobs, and two rented rooms with cooking privileges down the hall. My landlady, Mrs. Jefferson, was kind and grandmotherly. She was a ready babysitter and insisted on providing dinner for her tenants. Her ways were so tender and her personality so sweet that no one was mean enough to discourage her disastrous culinary exploits. Spaghetti at her table, which was offered at least three times a week, was a mysterious red, white, and brown concoction. We would occasionally encounter an unidentifiable piece of meat hidden among the pasta.

There was no money in my budget for restaurant food, so

I and my son Guy were often loyal, if unhappy, diners at Chez Jefferson.

My mother had moved from Post Street into a fourteen-room Victorian house on Fulton Street, which she filled with gothic, heavily carved furniture. The upholstery on the sofa and occasional chairs was red-wine-colored mohair. Oriental rugs were placed throughout the house. She had a live-in employee who cleaned the house and sometimes filled in as cook helper.

Mother picked up Guy twice a week and took him to her house where she fed him peaches and cream and hot dogs, but I only went to her house at our appointed time.

She understood and encouraged my self-reliance. We had a standing appointment, which I looked forward to eagerly. Once a month, she would cook one of my favorite dishes and I would go to her house. One lunch date stands out in my mind. I call it the Vivian's Red Rice Day.

When I arrived at the Fulton Street house my mother was dressed beautifully, her makeup was perfect, and she wore good jewelry.

After we embraced, I washed my hands and we walked through her formal dark dining room and into the large bright kitchen.

Much of lunch was already on the table. Vivian Baxter was very serious about her delicious meals.

On that long-ago Red Rice Day, my mother had placed on the table a crispy, dry-roasted capon, no dressing or gravy, and a simple lettuce salad, no tomatoes or cucumbers. A wide-mouthed bowl covered with a platter sat next to her plate.

She fervently blessed the food with a brief prayer and put her left hand on the platter and her right on the bowl. She turned the dishes over and gently loosened the bowl from its contents and revealed a tall mound of glistening red rice (my favorite food in all the world) decorated with finely minced parsley and the green stalks of scallions.

The chicken and salad do not feature so prominently on my taste buds' memory, but each grain of red rice is emblazoned on the surface of my tongue forever.

Gluttonous and *greedy* negatively describe the hearty eater offered the seduction of her favorite food.

Two large portions of rice sated my appetite, but the deliciousness of the dish made me long for a larger stomach so that I could eat two more helpings.

My mother had plans for the rest of the afternoon, so she gathered her wraps and we left the house together.

We reached the middle of the block and were enveloped in the stinging acid aroma of vinegar from the pickle factory on the corner of Fillmore and Fulton streets. I had walked ahead. My mother stopped me and said, "Baby."

I walked back to her.

"Baby, I've been thinking and now I am sure. You are the greatest woman I've ever met."

My mother was five feet four inches to my six-foot frame.

I looked down at the pretty little woman, and her perfect makeup and diamond earrings, who owned a hotel and was admired by most people in San Francisco's black community.

She continued, "You are very kind and very intelligent and those elements are not always found together. Mrs. Eleanor Roosevelt, Dr. Mary McLeod Bethune, and my mother—yes, you belong in that category. Here, give me a kiss."

She kissed me on the lips and turned and jaywalked across the street to her beige and brown Pontiac. I pulled myself together and walked down to Fillmore Street. I crossed there and waited for the number 22 streetcar.

My policy of independence would not allow me to accept money or even a ride from my mother, but I welcomed her wisdom. Now I thought of her statement. I thought, "Suppose she is right. She's very intelligent and she often said she didn't fear anyone enough to lie. Suppose I really am going to become somebody. Imagine."

At that moment, when I could still taste the red rice, I decided the time had come when I should cut down on dangerous habits like smoking, drinking, and cursing.

Imagine, I might really become somebody. Someday.

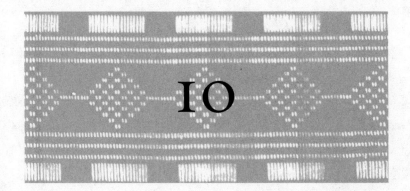

Morocco

Although I was living in the twentieth century, I still held on to the nineteenth-century fanciful idea of Arabia. There were Caliphs and strong sexless eunuchs and harems where beautiful women lay on chaise lounges looking at themselves in gilded mirrors.

On the first morning in Morocco, I went walking to soak up a little more romance to fit with my fantasies.

Some women in the street wore Western clothes, while others kept themselves chaste behind heavy black veils. All the men looked jaunty and handsome in their red fezzes. I approached a junkyard and decided to cross the street before I was forced to look at real life. Someone yelled and I turned. There were three tents in the yard and a few black men were waving at me. For the first time, I realized that the Moroccans I had met earlier and expected to meet resembled Spaniards or Mexicans rather than Africans.

The men were shouting and beckoning to me. I saw they were all very old. My upbringing told me that I had to go to them. At that moment I became aware that I was wearing a short skirt and high-heel shoes, appropriate for a twenty-five-year-old American woman, totally unacceptable for a female in the company of old African men.

I threaded my way over cans, broken bottles, and discarded furniture. When I reached the men, they sat down suddenly. There were no stools beneath them so they did not really sit, they simply squatted on their haunches. I was raised by a southern grandmother who taught me it was rude for a young person to stand or even sit taller than an older person.

When the men stooped, I stooped, I was a young dancer and my body followed my orders.

They smiled and spoke to me in a language that I could not understand. I responded in English, French, and Spanish, which they did not understand. We smiled at each other and one man spoke loudly to a group of women who were standing nearby, looking at me with interest.

I smiled at the women who returned my smile. Young trained muscles or not, stooping so long was becoming uncomfortable.

Just as I prepared to stand and bow, a woman appeared with a miniature coffee cup in her hand. She offered it to me. As I took it, I noticed two things, bugs crawling on the ground, and the men approving of me by snapping their fingers. I bowed and took a sip of the coffee and almost fainted. I had a cockroach on my tongue. I looked at the people's faces and I could not spit it out. My grandmother would have pushed away the grave's dirt and traveled by willpower to show me her face of abject disappointment. I could not bear that. I opened my throat and drank the cup dry. I counted four cockroaches.

Standing, I bowed to everyone and walked out of the yard. I held the revulsion until I cleared the lot, then I grabbed the first wall and let the nausea have its way. I did not tell the story to anyone; I was simply sick for one month.

When we performed in Marseilles I stayed in a cheap pensione. One morning I picked up a well-worn *Reader's Digest* and turned to an article called "African Tribes Traveling from the Sahel to North Africa."

I learned that many tribes who follow the old routes from Mali, Chad, Niger, Nigeria, and other Black African countries, crossing the Sahara en route to Mecca or Algeria or Morocco and the Sudan, carry little cash but live by the barter system. They swap goods for goods, but they will spend their scarce money to buy raisins. In order to honor and show respect to visitors, they will put three to five raisins into a small cup of coffee.

For a few minutes I felt that I wanted to stoop below the old men in Morocco and beg their pardon.

There, they had chosen to honor me with those expensive raisins.

I thanked God that my grandmother would have been pleased with my behavior.

I began this lifelong lesson. If human beings eat a thing, and if I am not so violently repelled by my own upbringing that I cannot speak, and if it is visually clean within reason, and if I am not allergic to the offering, I will sit at the table and with all the gusto I can manufacture I will join in the feast.

P.S. I call this a lifelong lesson for I have not fully learned it and I am often put to the test and although I am no more or less squeamish than the next person, I have sometimes earned a flat "F" at the test, failing miserably. But I get a passing grade more often than not. I just have to remember my grandmother and those four innocent raisins, which made me violently sick for one month.

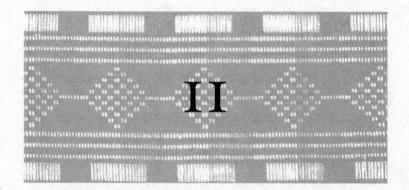

II

Porgy and Bess

Porgy and Bess, the George and Ira Gershwin opera, was still bringing audiences to their feet on its European tour. The colorful cast was still robust and welcoming to me but I was anxious to leave the tour and return to San Francisco, California.

I was riddled with guilt because when I joined the cast I had left my eight-year-old son Guy with my mother and an aunt in San Francisco.

The opera company offered me a sizeable increase in salary if I would send for him, but there were already two children traveling with their parents, who exhibited behavior that I did not want my son to see, nor imitate. I was principal dancer and sang the role "Ruby." I received a decent salary, which I sent home, but my guilt assured me that my money was not sufficient, so I stayed in pensiones or youth hostels, or with families to save money. After the curtain came down in the theater, I doubled singing the blues in nightclubs and in the daytime I taught dance wherever I could find students and I also sent that money to my mother.

Still, I began to lose my appetite and weight and interest in everything. I wanted to go home to my son. I was told that I was obliged to pay my replacement's fare to Europe and my own fare home. I met that new pressure by singing in two more nightclubs and teaching dance to professional dancers and to children barely able to walk.

At last I had the money and at last I boarded a ship in Naples, Italy, for New York. I refused to fly because it occurred to me if the plane crashed, my son would only be able to lament, "My mother died when I was eight years old. She was an entertainer." I had to get back to San Francisco and let him know that I was that and more.

After nine days on the ship I arrived in New York and took a train for three days and nights to San Francisco. Our reunion was so emotional that I confess it may have sent me over the edge. I know I loved my son and I knew I was blessed that I was not in love with him, that I would not smother him by trying to be too close, and at the same time I would love him and raise him to be free and manly and as happy as possible.

After one week of living in the top floor of my mother's big house, set on the top of a hill, I became anxious again. I realized it would be difficult if not impossible to raise a black boy to be happy and responsible and liberated in a racist society. I was lying on the sofa in the upstairs living room when Guy walked through. "Hello, Mom." I looked at him and thought I could pick him up, open the window and jump. I lifted my voice and said, "Get out. Get out now. Get out of the house this minute. Go out to the front yard and don't come back, even if I call you."

I telephoned for a taxi, walked down the steps and looked

at Guy. I said, "Now you may go in and please stay until I return." I told the cab driver to take me to Langley Porter Psychiatric Clinic. When I walked in the receptionist asked if I had an appointment. I said, "No." She explained with a sad face, "We cannot see you unless you have an appointment." I said, "I must see someone, I am about to hurt myself and maybe someone else."

The receptionist spoke quickly on the telephone. She said to me, "Please go to see Dr. Salsey, down the hall on the right, Room C." I opened the door of Room C and my hopes fell. There was a young white man behind a desk. He wore a Brooks Brothers suit and a button-down shirt and his face was calm with confidence. He welcomed me to a chair in front of his desk. I sat down and looked at him again and began to cry. How could this privileged young white man understand the heart of a black woman who was sick with guilt because she left her little black son for others to raise? Each time I looked up at him the tears flooded my face. Each time he asked what is the matter, how can I help you? I was maddened by the helplessness of my situation. Finally I was able to compose myself enough to stand up, thank him and leave. I thanked the receptionist and asked her to telephone Luxor Cab.

I went to my voice teacher, my mentor and the only person I could speak to openly. As I went up the stairs to Frederick Wilkerson's studio, I heard a student doing vocal exercises. Wilkie, as he was called, told me to go into the bedroom. "I am going to make you a drink." Leaving his student, he brought in a glass of Scotch, which I drank although at the time I was not a drinker. The liquor put me to sleep. When I awakened and heard no voices from the studio I went in.

Wilkie asked me, "What's wrong?"

I told him I was going crazy. He said no and then asked, "What's really wrong?" and I, upset that he had not heard me said, "I thought about killing myself today and killing Guy, I'm telling you I'm going crazy."

Wilkie said, "Sit down right here at this table, here is a yellow pad and here is a ballpoint pen. I want you to write down your blessings."

I said, "Wilkie, I don't want to talk about that, I'm telling you I am going crazy."

He said, "First write down that I said write down and think of the millions of people all over the world who cannot hear a choir, or a symphony, or their own babies crying. Write down, I can hear—Thank God. Then write down that you can see this yellow pad, and think of the millions of people around the world who cannot see a waterfall, or flowers blooming, or their lover's face. Write I can see—Thank God. Then write down that you can read. Think of the millions of people around the world who cannot read the news of the day, or a letter from home, a stop sign on a busy street, or . . ."

I followed Wilkie's orders and when I reached the last line on the first page of the yellow pad, the agent of madness was routed.

That incident took place over fifty years ago. I have written some twenty-five books, maybe fifty articles, poems, plays, and speeches all using ballpoint pens and writing on yellow pads.

When I decide to write anything, I get caught up in my insecurity despite the prior accolades. I think, uh, uh, now they will know I am a charlatan that I really cannot write and write really well. I am almost undone, then I pull out a new yellow pad and as I approach the clean page, I think of how blessed I am.

The ship of my life may or may not be sailing on calm and amiable seas. The challenging days of my existence may or may not be bright and promising. Stormy or sunny days, glorious or lonely nights, I maintain an attitude of gratitude. If I insist on being pessimistic, there is always tomorrow.

Today I am blessed.

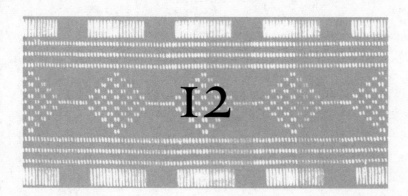

12

Bob & Decca

Bob Treuhaft and Decca Mitford were among the most engaging couples I had ever known. He was a radical lawyer, of steely resolve, with bones so delicate that once, after successfully defending the Black Panthers, Huey Newton gave him a grateful embrace and broke three of his ribs.

Decca was a writer whose book *Hons and Rebels* reveals her story of growing up as an English aristocrat and becoming a communist.

Her next book, *The American Way of Death,* challenged and changed the funeral business in America.

I accepted an invitation to speak at Stanford University. Since I could visit Decca and Bob, I added a weekend onto the trip.

On the first night together, Bob said that once a month a local restaurant offered a French bistro menu with only two seatings per night. He said the food was exquisite and so popular that people reserved two to three months ahead.

Decca asked Bob to call and tell the owner Bruce Marshall that they had a close writer friend visiting from New York. Bob came back with a smile and we had a booking.

As we were seated at a table a measure wider than a dinner plate, the owner came over to us.

He said to me, "My wife was so excited to know you were in town, you and she are great friends."

I thanked him and asked first, how did he know that I was in town? He said Bob Treuhaft had told him. He had even described me.

Then I asked of his wife. Bruce said that his wife was Marilyn Marshall. I ran my mind over a list of names. I knew no Marilyn Marshall.

He saw my quandary and laughed at himself, "No, of course, she was a Greene when you knew each other, in Los Angeles." I did know a family in Los Angeles with the last name Greene, but there was no Marilyn in the group. He laughed again and brought a wallet from his pocket. He flipped it open and handed the wallet to me. "Here is Marilyn's photo." Names and places may change but unless one has had extreme cosmetic surgery, the features remain the same. I gave the photo a hurried look. I had never seen that woman's face before.

I smiled and said, "That is certainly Marilyn Marshall. She looks great."

Bruce gave our table the grin of a proud groom.

As we were leaving, Bruce caught us at the front door. "Marilyn is on the phone and she wants to speak to you."

I held the earphone tight on my ear, hoping that the voice would offer cognition.

I said, "Hello," and was truly disappointed. I didn't recognize the voice.

She asked, "What are you doing in California? Why didn't you let me know you were coming? If we didn't live so far, I'd come to the restaurant right now."

Hurriedly I said, "No, we are already finished. What about tomorrow? Come around one o'clock for lunch at Decca Mitford and Bob Treuhaft's. I'll make a quiche."

She said, "I'll be there."

When I told Decca that I needed her to be present, she said, "Not for a minute."

I asked, "What will I talk about?"

Decca said, "You have the quiche, talk about that."

I put a quiche Lorraine in the oven and tried to imagine the next two hours.

At exactly one o'clock the doorbell rang, and I opened the door to a woman I had never seen in my life. She was petite and pretty and surprise was plastered on her face. "Hey, how are you?"

I said, "Wonderful. What about you? Come in."

She did.

I told her the quiche was ready and she said so was she. We sat together knowing that neither had any idea who the other was, or how to extricate ourselves from the awkward situation.

After lunch we had a long conversation on making quiche Lorraine. We took our wine to the living room.

Marilyn said, "Guess who I saw up in Tahoe?"

I said I couldn't guess.

She said, "Charles Chestnut. He acted as if he did not recognize me."

She half expected me to know the name and also not to recognize it at all. I was not as courageous as she. I said nothing.

Marilyn continued, "I spoke to him and he kept looking at me quizzically. I thought, the bastard. As hard as you and I worked in his campaign." Again, I had no response.

Marilyn said, "I walked up to him and said, you're pretending not to know me now, wait until I see Louise Meriwether."

Aha. Here was the answer to my questions.

"Marilyn, I hate to tell you this, but I am not Louise Meriwether."

She shouted, "I didn't think you were! I didn't recognize your voice last night on the telephone."

She was standing in the middle of the room. "And when you opened the door I thought, that's not Louise unless she did something drastic to herself."

I asked, "Why did you think I was Louise?"

Marilyn said, "Bruce told me that Bob Treuhaft told him that you, Louise, were visiting from New York and he knows how much I care about you, I mean Louise."

She asked, "Please tell me, who are you?"

I said, "Maya Angelou."

Marilyn said, "Oh hell, listen I'll just go, I'm sorry."

I said, "No, please, this is just a new way of making a friend. Let's figure out what happened."

She said, "Bob called Bruce, hoping to get a reservation. He said they had a friend staying with them, an African American writer from New York."

Bruce asked, "Is she tall?"

Bob answered, "She's six feet."

Louise Meriwether is six-feet tall, black, and a writer.

And Bruce said, "That's my wife's dear friend."

Obviously there was only one six-foot tall black female writer in New York.

Marilyn and I shared a laugh of delight at the expense of men who know everything and at ourselves who nearly pulled off a non-visit between strangers.

She was a psychologist and a writer. I saw that she was my kind of person. Smart, funny, and tough-minded, and she became a friend to me in a way I could not anticipate.

My beloved brother Bailey had fought heroin for control of his life. The battle still raged but he told me he sincerely wanted to be drug free. I offered to pay for sessions with two of the leading black male psychologists in the area, but he refused.

I talked to him about Marilyn Marshall and he picked up one of her books and read it. That was typical of Bailey—drugs or no drugs—he would do his homework. He said he would like to meet her.

I told Marilyn all of this and she agreed to see him, not as a patient, but as the brother of a friend. I spoke to Bruce Marshall and arranged for Bailey to eat lunch and dinner at his restaurant. He could bring a guest and sign the bill. Only Bruce, Marilyn, and I would know that he was not paying. Bailey made use of the restaurant and had occasional conversations with Marilyn Greene Marshall.

So, for a year my brother was able to control his life. I have given great thanks for the help of two strangers I met by comic accident. I learned that a friend may be waiting behind a stranger's face.

Celia Cruz

There are certain artists who belong to all the people, everywhere, all the time.

The list of singers, musicians, and poets must include David the harpist from the Old Testament, Aesop the Storyteller, Omar Khayyam the Tent Maker, Shakespeare the Bard of Avon, Louis Armstrong the genius of New Orleans, Om Kalsoum the soul of Egypt, Frank Sinatra, Mahalia Jackson, Dizzy Gillespie, Ray Charles . . .

The names could go on until there was no breath to announce them, but the name of Celia Cruz, the great Cuban singer will always figure among them as one who belonged to all people. Her songs in Spanish were weighted with sympathy for the human spirit.

In the early 1950s I first listened to a Celia Cruz record, and although I spoke Spanish fairly well and loved her music, I found it hard to translate. I went on a search for everything about Celia Cruz and realized that if I was to become her devoted fan, I had to study Spanish more diligently. I did.

I enlisted the help of my brother Bailey in New York to find every record she ever made and every magazine that mentioned her name. My Spanish improved. Years later when I worked with Tito Puente, Willie BoBo, and Mongo Santamaría, I could hold my own onstage as well as in conversation with them backstage.

I had begun singing professionally, but my singing left a lot to be desired. I held my own onstage because my rhythms were exciting. Some I had grown up with and others I had found and lifted whole and wholly from the records of Celia Cruz.

Cruz came to the United States and played in a theater on Upper Broadway in New York City and I went to see her every day of her stay. She exploded on the stage and was sensual and touchingly present. From her, I learned to bring everything I had onto the stage with me. And now, some forty-plus years later, without music and by simply reading, I am able to read poetry and satisfy audiences. Much of the presence I bring to my performance, I learned from Celia Cruz.

All great artists draw from the same resource: the human heart, which tells us all that we are more alike than we are unalike.

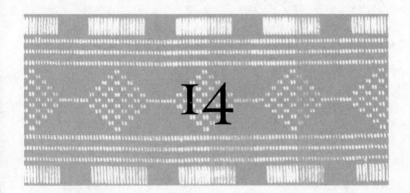

Fannie Lou Hamer

"All of this on account we want to register, to become first-class citizens, and if the Freedom Democratic Party is not seated now, I question America, is this America, the land of the free and the home of the brave, where we have to sleep with our telephones off the hooks because our lives be threatened daily because we want to live as decent human beings, in America? Thank you."
—FANNIE LOU HAMER

It is important that we know that those words came from the lips of an African American woman. It is imperative that we know those words come from the heart of an American.

I believe that there lives a burning desire in the most sequestered private heart of every American, a desire to belong to a great country. I believe that every citizen wants to stand on the world stage and represent a noble country where the mighty do not always crush the weak and the dream of a democracy is not the sole possession of the strong.

We must hear the questions raised by Fannie Lou Hamer forty years ago. Every American everywhere asks herself, himself, these questions Hamer asked:

What do I think of my country? What is there, which elevates my shoulders and stirs my blood when I hear the words, the United States of America: Do I praise my country enough? Do I laud my fellow citizens enough? What is there about my country that makes me hang my head and avert my eyes when I hear the words the United States of America, and what am I doing about it? Am I relating my disappointment to my leaders and to my fellow citizens, or am I like someone not involved, sitting high and looking low? As Americans, we should not be afraid to respond.

We have asked questions down a pyramid of years and given answers, which our children memorize, and which have become an integral part of the spoken American history.

Patrick Henry remarked, "I know not what course others may take, but as for me, give me liberty or give me death."

George Moses Horton, the nineteenth century poet, born a slave, said, "Alas, and was I born for this, to wear this brutish chain? I must slash the handcuffs from my wrists and live a man again."

> "The thought of only being a creature of the present and the past was troubling. I longed for a future too, with hope in it. The desire to be free, awakened my determination to act, to think, and to speak."
> —FREDERICK DOUGLASS

The love of democracy motivated Harriet Tubman to seek and find not only her own freedom, but to make innumerable trips to the slave South to gain the liberty of many slaves and instill the idea into the hearts of thousands that freedom is possible.

Fannie Lou Hamer and the Mississippi Democratic Freedom Party were standing on the shoulders of history when they acted to unseat evil from its presumed safe perch on the backs of the American people. It is fitting to honor the memory of Fannie Lou Hamer and surviving members of the Mississippi Democratic Freedom Party. For their gifts to us, we say thank you.

The human heart is so delicate and sensitive that it always needs some tangible encouragement to prevent it from faltering in its labor. The human heart is so robust, so tough, that once encouraged it beats its rhythm with a loud unswerving insistency. One thing that encourages the heart is music. Throughout the ages we have created songs to grow on and to live by. We Americans have created music to embolden the hearts and inspire the spirit of people all over the world.

Fannie Lou Hamer knew that she was one woman and only one woman. However, she knew she was an American, and as an American she had a light to shine on the darkness of racism. It was a little light, but she aimed it directly at the gloom of ignorance.

Fannie Lou Hamer's favorite was a simple song that we all know. We Americans have sung it since childhood . . .

> *"This little light of mine,*
> *I'm going to let it shine,*
> *Let it shine,*
> *Let it shine,*
> *Let it shine."*

Senegal

Samia was a famous actress from Senegal who dressed in glamorous flowing clothes. I met her on a trip to Paris. She and her French husband, Pierre, were members of a group of artistic intellectuals who drank barrels of cheap wine and who discussed everything and everybody, from Nietzsche to James Baldwin.

I fitted into the Parisian assemblage comfortably. We all preened about our youth and talent and intelligence as if we had created the gifts ourselves, for ourselves.

Samia said she and her husband lived most of the year in Dakar, the capital of Senegal, and I would always be welcome in their home. Years passed before I did visit Senegal, but the telephone number they had given me still worked. I was invited for dinner.

I entered a beautifully furnished living room to the sound of people laughing and glasses clinking with ice. The guests were integrated. As many Europeans as Africans were enjoying a full-blown party. Samia introduced me to a small group near the door and stayed talking to us until a server offered me a drink.

I wandered from group to group. Samia's first language was Serer but I did not speak Serer and the Senegalese accent made the French which was spoken, hard for me to comprehend. I passed an open door where people stood along the wall, careful not to step on the beautiful Oriental rug in the center of the room.

I had known a woman in Egypt who would not allow her servants to walk on her rugs saying that only she, her family and friends were going to wear out her expensive carpets. Samia plummeted in my estimation. Obviously she had informed her guests that she would not look favorably on them if they stepped on her rug. I wondered what words did one use to inform a guest how to behave? I decided to find out.

I went into the room and in the guise of looking closely at some paintings on the wall, I walked across the center of the rug, then turned and walked back to another painting. I must have stepped on the rug four or five times. The guests who were bunched up on the sidelines smiled at me weakly. They might be encouraged to admit that rugs were to be walked on.

A Senegalese woman in a white brocade gown smiled at me and engaged me in conversation. She was a writer and we began talking about books. I became so interested I nearly missed the next scene. Two maids came and rolled up the rug I had walked on and took it away. They returned immediately with another equally as beautiful. They spread it, and patted it until it was smooth.

They then put glasses on the carpet and huge serving spoons, folded napkins and silverware, wine and pitchers of water. Finally a bowl of steaming rice and chicken was placed on the carpet.

Samia and Pierre appeared and clapping their hands they called for attention. Samia announced that they were serving the most popular Senegalese dish, "Yassah, for our sister from America." She waved her hand at me and said, "For Maya Angelou" adding, "Shall we sit?"

All the guests sank to the floor. My face and neck burned. Fortunately, because of my chocolate brown complexion, people could not know I was on fire with shame. Clever and so proper Maya Angelou, I had walked up and down over the tablecloth.

I sat, but I found swallowing hard to do. The food had to force its way over that knot of embarrassment.

In an unfamiliar culture, it is wise to offer no innovations, no suggestions, or lessons.

The epitome of sophistication is utter simplicity.

16

The Eternal Silver Screen

Many years have passed since the American Film Institute gave a tribute to William Wyler, one of Hollywood's most prolific and prestigious directors. I, as a member of the Board of Trustees, was asked to participate in the ceremony. I was to make a simple introduction. Of course I was flattered by the invitation and I accepted.

The affair, held at the posh Century Plaza Hotel, was attended by the most glamorous and famous actors and actresses of the day. Fred Astaire was there, as well as Audrey Hepburn and Gregory Peck. Walter Pidgeon, Greer Garson, Henry Fonda, and Charlton Heston sparkled in the audience. I sat trembling at a table and looked around the room. These were some of the faces which formed my ideas of romance, dignity, and justice. These people on the silver screen had shown grace, morality and beauty, chivalry and courage. Then the picture of the segregated movie house in my small town in Arkansas floated into my consciousness.

Each time my brother and I had gone to a picture show, we had to brave the hostile stares of white adults, and once gaining the box office, we paid our money and were rudely thumbed toward a rickety outdoor staircase which led to the balcony (called a buzzard's roost) restricted to black customers.

There we sat, knees to chin, in the cramped space, our feet crunching discarded candy wrappers and other debris on the floor. We perched there and studied how to act when we grew up and became beautiful and rich and white.

Years had passed and now I sat in the hotel's glittery ball-room and watched as movie star after movie star rose to pay tribute to Mr. Wyler. Old memories had taken me back to days of Southern humiliation. When my name was called, every word of my carefully memorized introduction fled from my mind, and I stood at the microphone looking into the famous faces, furious that they had been, even unwittingly, the agents of my old embarrassments. Anger thickened my tongue and slowed my brain. Only by exercising phenomenal control did I restrain myself from shouting, "I hate you. I hate you all. I hate you for your power and fame, and health and money, and acceptance." I think I was afraid that if I opened my mouth I would blurt out the truth: "I love you because I love everything you've got and everything you are." I stood mute before the famed audience. After a few attempts to speak I mumbled a few words and walked out of the room.

There was a rumor—which was untrue—that drugs had made me blank out. Upon later reflection of the painful inci-dent, I am remembering what Arkansas gave me. I came to understand that I can never forget where I came from. My soul should always look back and wonder at the mountains I had climbed and the rivers I had forged and the challenges which still await down the road. I am strengthened by that knowledge.

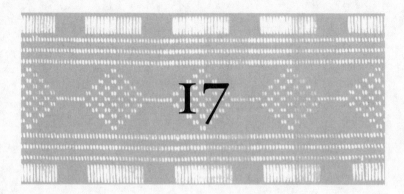

17

In Self-Defense

Recently I had an appointment with four television producers who wanted my permission to produce a short story I had written.

As often happens, the leader of the group showed herself immediately. There was no question as to who was the boss. The woman was small, with a quick smile and a high-pitched voice. She met each statement I made with a sarcastic rejoinder. Not caustic enough for me to call her down but pointed enough for me to realize she meant to put me in my place, which was obviously somewhere beneath her.

I said, "I'm glad we are meeting in this restaurant, it is one of my favorites."

She said, "I have not been here for years but I remember the last time the atmosphere was so boring we could have been in an old lady's home."

She looked around, smirked, and said, "It does not seem as if it has gotten any better."

After she had responded sarcastically to my statements three times, I asked, "Why are you doing that?"

She answered in a sweet innocent voice, "What, what am I doing?"

I said, "You are timidly attacking me."

She laughed and said, "Oh no, I was just showing you that you cannot be right about everything all the time. Anyway, I like to have a little word warfare going on. It sharpens the wit, and I am brutally frank."

I kept my hands in my lap and brought my chin to my chest. I ordered myself to be kind.

I asked the producer, "Word warfare? Do you really want to call me out into the arena for word warfare?"

And she said boldly, "Yes, I do, yes, I do, yes, I do."

"No, I do not, but let us speak about the business which brought us together. Your corporation wanted my permission to explore my short story as a vehicle for television. I must tell you no. I will not agree."

She said, "We have not even made our offer to you."

I told her, "That does not matter. I know very well that you would not furnish me a peaceful or pleasant environment in which to work. That is not how you work, so I am obliged to refuse any offer you might make."

I thought I could have added, "I promise you, you do not want me as your adversary, because once I feel myself under threat, I fight to win, and in that case I will forget that I am thirty years older than you, with a reputation for being passionate. Then after the fray, if I see I have vanquished you, I would be embarrassed that I have brought all the pain, brought all the joy, brought all the fear and the glory that I have lived through, to triumph over a single woman who did not know that she should be careful of who she calls out, and I would not like myself very much. And if you bested me, I would be devastated and might start to throw things."

I am never proud to participate in violence, yet I know that each of us must care enough for ourselves that we can be ready and able to come to our own defense when and wherever needed.

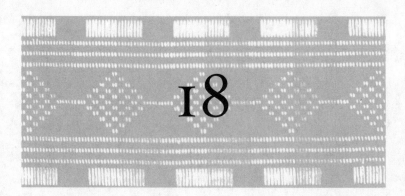

18

Mrs. Coretta Scott King

Over the last few years, and even in the last few months, I have said reluctant goodbyes to friends I have known over forty years. Friends I miss, with whom I learned many of life's sweetest and most painful lessons.

I still miss James Baldwin and Alex Haley and the loud talking, shouting, laughing, crying weekends that we shared. Betty Shabazz is near enough for me to remember what she was wearing when I last cooked dinner for her. Tom Feelings and I produced a book together and he drew a portrait of my late mother, which hangs in my bedroom. I spoke to Ossie Davis a few days before he died and agreed to stand in for him and his wife, Ruby Dee, at an engagement they could not cover in Washington, D.C.

And recently, I waved farewell to Coretta Scott King, a chosen sister. As I approach my birthday every year, I am reminded that Martin Luther King was assassinated on my birthday and each year for the last thirty years, Coretta Scott King and I have sent flowers or cards to each other or shared telephone calls on April 4.

I find it very difficult to let a friend or beloved go into that country of no return. I answer the heroic question, "Death, where is thy sting?" with "It is here in my heart, and my mind, and my memories."

I am besieged with painful awe at the vacuum left by the dead. Where did she go? Where is he now? Are they, as the poet James Weldon Johnson said, "resting in the bosom of Jesus"? If so, what about my Jewish loves, my Japanese dears, and my Muslim darlings. Into whose bosom are they cuddled?

I find relief from the questions only when I concede that I am not obliged to know everything. I remind myself it is sufficient to know what I know, and that what I know, may not always be true.

When I find myself filling with rage over the loss of a beloved, I try as soon as possible to remember that my concerns and questions should be focused on what I learned or what I have yet to learn from my departed love. What legacy was left which can help me in the art of living a good life?

Did I learn to be kinder,
To be more patient,
And more generous,
More loving,
More ready to laugh,
And more easy to accept honest tears?
If I accept those legacies of my departed beloveds, I am able to
    say, Thank You to them for their love and Thank You to
    God for their lives.

19

Condolences

For a too brief moment in the universe the veil was lifted. The mysterious became known. Questions met answers somewhere behind the stars. Furrowed brows were smoothed and eyelids closed over long unblinking stares.

Your beloved occupied the cosmos. You awoke to sunrays and nestled down to sleep in moonlight. All life was a gift open to you and burgeoning for you. Choirs sang to harps and your feet moved to ancestral drumbeats. *For you were sustaining and being sustained by the arms of your beloved.*

Now the days stretch before you with the dryness and sameness of desert dunes. And in this season of grief we who love you have become invisible to you. Our words worry the empty air around you and you can sense no meaning in our speech.

Yet, we are here. We are still here. Our hearts ache to support you.

We are always loving you.

You are not alone.

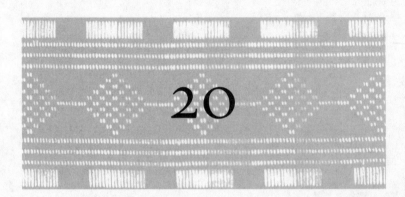

20

In the Valley of Humility

In the early seventies I was invited to speak at Wake Forest University in Winston-Salem. The school had only recently been integrated.

I told my husband that the visit interested me. He was a master builder and had just signed a large contract so he could not accompany me. I called my close friend in New York. Dolly McPherson said she would meet me in Washington, D.C., and we could travel south together.

My lecture was well received at the school and before I could leave the building, the students came up to me and asked me to meet with them.

I went with Dolly to the student lounge where there, the students crowded in on every sofa, chair, stool, and pillow on the floor. They were pointedly separate with the black students seated down front in a group.

There was no hesitation in offering questions. One young white male said, "I am nineteen, I am going to be a man, but strictly speaking, I'm still a boy. But that guy there"—he pointed to the black student—"gets mad if I call him boy, and we're the same age. Why is that?" I waved at the black student. "There he is, why not ask him?"

A black female student said, "I went to a good high school where I graduated valedictorian. I speak good English. Why do they"—she nodded to the white students—"think I need them to speak to me in accents so thick I can hardly understand?"

I asked her to tell me how she was spoken to. She said, "They say, 'Hey y'all, how y'all doin'? Y'all okay?'" She spoke with such an extreme exaggerated Southern accent that everyone laughed.

I said, "They are right there, why don't you ask them?" As they began talking to one another, I realized that I was being used as a bridge. The parents of those students had never had a language, that allowed them to speak to one another as equals, and now their children were creating a way that would allow them to have a dialogue. I sat with them until midnight, encouraging, abetting, and urging them to speak.

When I stood, exhausted, Tom Mullin, the Dean of Wake Forest College, came to me with an offer: "Dr. Angelou, if ever you want to retire, we welcome you to Wake Forest University. We will gladly make a place for you." I thanked him politely, knowing that I would never come to the South to live.

The next morning, Dolly and I were taken to the airport early enough to have breakfast in the cafe. We were given a table and ordered breakfast. We sat unserved for more than thirty minutes. I noticed that she and I were the only black customers in the restaurant.

I told Dolly, "Sister, prepare to go to jail, because if these people don't want to serve us I am going to turn the place out."

She said calmly, "All right, Sis."

I called the waitress over, a lanky young white woman. I said, "My sister ordered a cheese omelet and I ordered bacon and eggs, thirty minutes ago. If you don't want to serve us, I advise you to tell me so, and then call the police."

The young woman was immediately solicitous. Speaking in her soft North Carolina accent she said, "No ma'am, it's not that, it's just that the chef run out of grits. He can't serve breakfast without grits. See, half of the people on this side are not eating. The grits will be ready in about ten minutes and then I will serve you." She pronounced the word "grits" as if it had two syllables—"gri-its."

I felt the ninny of all times. My face became hot and my neck burned. I apologized to the waitress somehow, and Dolly McPherson controlled herself and did not mention my stupidity. When I returned to my sturdy home and steady husband, I told everyone about the school, the students and the offer. I did not mention the airport drama.

I was married to Paul DuFeu, a master builder, a writer, and a popular cartoonist in England. Within two days of our meeting we knew we were in love together and had to be in life together.

For ten years we surprised, amused, angered, and supported each other. Unexpectedly a storm cloud roared into that sunny climate of love. My queries annoyed him, my husband admitted that he had grown weary of monogamy and needed more provocation in his life.

We separated just as I was to begin a national lecture tour. Since my husband was a builder and his business was based in northern California, I decided to make him a gift of San Francisco and the bridges and the hills, and the gourmet restaurants and the beautiful bay view.

Divorce like every other rite of passage introduces new landscapes, new rhythms, new faces and places, and sometimes races.

I fulfilled my lecture engagements around the country, meanwhile looking for a safe and soft place to fall. As a writer I should be able to pick up my yellow pads, ballpoint pens, Random House dictionary, Roget's Thesaurus, King James Bible, a deck of playing cards, and a bottle of good sherry and write anywhere. Denver, Colorado, was beautiful, but its air too raw, and while there were some black people, Latinos, and Native Americans, the city itself was not integrated. I looked at Chattanooga, Tennessee, but a large portion of its population was still actively arrayed on the Confederate side in the ongoing Civil War.

Other cities I visited were either too large and/or too small and insular. Cambridge, Massachusetts, seemed to have all I wanted, history, universities, a mixture of races, great bookstores, churches, and places to party on Saturday night. Only Winston-Salem, North Carolina, with all the same assets, vied with Cambridge. I visited both towns twice.

I finally released Cambridge because I am a southern woman who does not do snow with any grace, and each year Cambridge, Massachusetts, has more snow than would make me comfortable.

Once I was settled in Winston-Salem, Dr. Ed Wilson, provost of the university, and Dr. Tom Mullin, who had offered me a position a decade earlier, came to me and offered a Reynolds Professorship with a lifetime appointment. I thanked them and said I would take it for a year to see if I liked teaching, and indeed if I liked Winston-Salem.

Within three months of teaching, I had an enormous revelation; I realized I was not a writer who teaches, but a teacher who writes.

On earlier visits to North Carolina, I had made friends with the chairman of the English Department, Elizabeth Phillips, and other faculty members. On evenings after dinner and afternoons after lunch, I asked them questions, which had befuddled me. I needed to know how had they accepted the idea of segregation? Did they really believe that black people were inferior to whites? Did they think that black people were born with a contagious ailment, which made it dangerous to sit next to us on buses while allowing us to cook their meals and even breast-feed their babies?

I was heartened to hear my new colleagues answer me with candor, honesty, embarrassment, and some contrition. "Truly, I didn't think about it. It had always been and it seemed it would always be." "I did think about it but I didn't think there was anything I could do to change the situation." "When the black youngsters protested by sitting at the 5 & Dime store counter in Greensboro, I was so proud. I remember wishing that I was black and I could go join them."

Whether I liked it or not I had to admit that I understood the sense of helplessness of my colleagues. Their responses confirmed my belief that courage is the most important of all the virtues. I thought, had I been white during the segregation era, I also might have taken the line of least resistance.

I began healing when I settled in Winston-Salem. The undulating landscape is replete with flowering dogwood, redbud, crepe myrtle trees, six-foot-tall rhododendron. Multicolored four-foot-wide azaleas grow wild and wonderful throughout the area.

Winston-Salem is in the Piedmont, it is literally at the foot of the mountains. The mountains that lean over us are the Great Smokies and the Blue Ridge. I like the humor in North Carolina. The natives say that our state is the valley of humility, towered over by two towers of conceit, Virginia and South Carolina.

I was happy to find good museums, excellent churches with choirs to match, a first-class school of the arts, which supplied stars for Broadway plays and a violinist chair for the New York Symphony.

I fell for the soft singing accent of the natives and their creative ways with English. In the supermarket the checker asked me how did I like Winston-Salem? I replied, "I like it, but it gets so hot. I don't know if I can bear it."

The checker, not breaking her stride in totaling my items said to me, "Yes, Dr. Angelou, but it gone get gone."

I found and joined Mt. Zion Baptist Church with its great choirs and devoted minister. There is nearby a principal and training hospital for the town. One of my colleagues focused her interest on Emily Dickinson and another on eighteenth- and nineteenth-century European poetry, which meant I could find friends to discuss poetry, one of my most favorite subjects.

Winston-Salem is not without difficulties. Racism still rages behind many smiling faces, and women are still spoken of in some circles, as conveniently pretty vessels. My late friend John O. Killens once said to me, "Macon, Georgia, is down south, New York City is up south."

Blithering ignorance can be found wherever you choose to live.

The late nineteenth- and twentieth-century great African

American poet, Anne Spencer, loved Virginia and loved Robert Browning. She wrote a poem, "Life-Long, Poor Browning . . ."

"Heaven's Virginia when the year's at its Spring."

That may be so of Virginia. I know it is so of North Carolina and of Winston-Salem in particular.

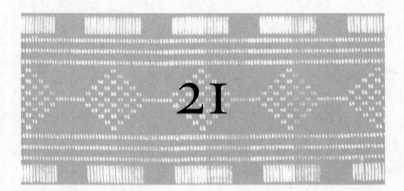

21

National Spirit

For the past four decades our national spirit and natural joy have ebbed. Our national expectations have diminished. Our hope for the future has waned to such a degree that we risk sneers and snorts of derision when we confess that we are hoping for bright tomorrows.

How have we come so late and lonely to this place? When did we relinquish our desire for a high moral ground to those who clutter our national landscape with vulgar accusations and gross speculations?

Are we not the same people who have fought a war in Europe to eradicate an Aryan threat to murder an entire race? Have we not worked, prayed, planned to create a better world? Are we not the same citizens who struggled, marched, and went to jail to obliterate legalized racism from our country? Didn't we dream of a country where freedom was in the national conscience and dignity was the goal?

We must insist that the men and women who expect to

lead us recognize the true desires of those who are being led. We do not choose to be herded into a building burning with hate nor into a system rife with intolerance.

Politicians must set their aims for the high ground and according to our various leanings, Democratic, Republican, Independent, we will follow.

Politicians must be told if they continue to sink into the mud of obscenity, they will proceed alone.

If we tolerate vulgarity, our future will sway and fall under a burden of ignorance. It need not be so. We have the brains and the heart to face our futures bravely. Taking responsibility for the time we take up and the space we occupy. To respect our ancestors and out of concern for our descendants, we must show ourselves as courteous and courageous well-meaning Americans.

Now.

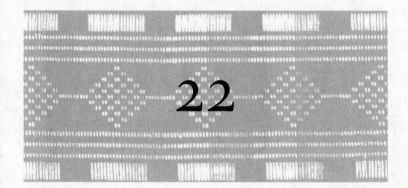

22

Reclaiming Southern Roots

After generations of separations and decades of forgetfulness, the mention of the South brings back to our memories ancient years of pain and pleasure. At the turn of the twentieth century, many African Americans left the Southern towns, left the crushing prejudice and prohibition, and moved north to Chicago and New York City, west to Los Angeles and San Diego.

They were drawn by the heady promise of better lives, of equality, fair play, and good old American four-star freedom. Their expectations were at once fulfilled and at the same time dashed to the ground and broken into shards of disappointment.

The sense of fulfillment arose from the fact that there were chances to exchange the dull drudgery of sharecrop farming for protected work under unionized agreements. Sadly for the last thirty years, those jobs have been decreasing as industry became computerized and work was sent to foreign countries.

The climate which the immigrants imagined as free of racial prejudice was found to be discriminatory in ways different from the Southern modes and possibly even more humiliating.

A small percentage of highly skilled and fully educated blacks found and clung to rungs on the success ladder. Unskilled and undereducated black workers were spit out by the system like so many undigestible watermelon seeds.

They began to find their lives minimalized, and their selves as persons trivialized. Many members of that early band of twentieth-century pilgrims must have yearned for the honesty of Southern landscapes where even if they were the targets of hate mongers who wanted them dead, they were at least credited with being alive. Northern whites with their public smiles of liberal acceptance and their private behavior of utter rejection wearied and angered the immigrants.

They stayed, however, in big city hovels, crowded into small tenements, and flowing out to the mean and quickly criminal street. They raised children who were sent south each summer to visit grandparents, third cousins, double second cousins and extended families. Those children grew up, mainly in the large Northern cities, with memories now dead, of Southern summers, fish fries, Saturday barbecues, and the gentle manners of Southern upbringing. These are the people who are coming back to the South to live. They often find that their Southern relatives have died or have themselves been transplanted to Detroit or Cleveland, Ohio. Still they come to live in Atlanta— "Y'all like Hot Lanta?"—and New Orleans, quickly learning to call the historic city by its rightful name of "N'awlins."

They return to the South to find or make places for themselves in the land of their foreparents. They make friends under the shade of trees their ancestors left decades earlier.

Many find themselves happy, without being able to explain the emotion. I think it is simply that they feel generally important. Southern themes will range from generous and luscious love to cruel and bitter hate, but no one can ever claim that the South is petty or indifferent. Even in little Stamps, Arkansas, black people walk with an air which implies "when I walk in, they may like me or dislike me, but everybody knows I'm here."

23

Surviving

Where the winds of disappointment
dash my dream house to the ground
and anger, octopus-like, wraps its tentacles around my soul
I just stop myself. I stop in my tracks
and look for one thing that can
heal me.
I find in my memory
one child's face
any child's face
looking at a desired toy
with sweet surprise
a child's face
with hopeful expectation in his eyes

The second I realize I am gazing at a face
sweet with youth and innocence, I am drawn away

from gloom and despair, and into the pleasing climate
of hope.

Each time my search for true love
leads me to the gates of hell
where Satan waits with open arms
I imagine the laughter of women friends,
their sounds tinkle like wind charms
urged by a searching breeze
I remember the sturdy guffaw of happy men and
my feet, without haste, and with purpose
move past the threatening open gates
to an area, secure from the evil of heartbreak

I am a builder
Sometimes I have built well, but often
I have built without researching the ground
upon which I put my building
I raised a beautiful house
and I lived in it for a year
Then it slowly drifted away with the tides
for I had laid the foundation
upon shifting sand

Another time I erected a
mansion, the windows shining
like mirrors
and the walls were hung
with rich tapestry, but
the earth shook with a

slight tremor, and the walls gave way, the floors opened
and my castle fell into pieces around my feet

The emotional sway of events and the impermanence
of construction echo the ways of dying love.

I have found that the platonic affection
in friendships and the familial
love for children can be relied upon
with certainty to lift the bruised soul
and repair the wounded spirit
and I am finished with
erotic romance.

Until . . .

24

Salute to Older Lovers

A sixty-five-year-old woman friend recently married a fifty-two-year-old man. At the ceremony there were many faces stiff with disapproval. What did he want marrying her? Weren't there young women properly three or four years younger than he? And what did she mean marrying him? In ten years, osteoporosis will ride her back without a saddle, and arthritis will disfigure her hands. If she could not find a mate when she was younger, she should just give up, give in, and give over to old age and loneliness.

And what did I think? I said, "I commend lovers, I am enheartened by lovers, I am encouraged by their courage and inspired by their passion."

I have come to speak of love
of its valleys and its hills
its tremors, chills and thrills
I have come to say I love love
and I love loving love

and I, surely, love
the brave and sturdy hearts
who dare to love.
Today, these lovers
have broken the bonds of timidity
and stepped out
before the entire world to say,
*   "See us, family and friends*
*   denying none of the years*
*   which have branded our bodies*
*   and none of the past broken vows*
*   which have seared our souls.*
*   You may think this undertaking*
*   Should be left to younger hearts*
*   But love has given us the courage to venture*
*   boldly into the sacred country of*
*   marriage, admitting our wrinkles,*
*   we allow them to*
*   show themselves bravely*
*   and our bones know the weight*
*   of the years.*
*   Yet we dare*
*   face down loneliness*
*   and embrace the*
*   uplifting communion*
*   found in a good marriage.*
*   We dare and we hope."*

They are blessed by love, and each of us on whom their love
light beams is enriched.
Thank you, Lovers.

25

Commencement Address

And now the work begins
And now the joy begins
Now the years of preparation
Of tedious study and
Exciting learning
are explained.

The jumble of words and
Tangle of great and small ideas
Begin to take order and
This morning you can see
A small portion of the large
Plan of your futures.

Your hours of application,
The hopes of your parents,
And the labor of your instructors

Have all brought this moment
Into your hands.

Today, you are princesses and princes
Of the morning.
Ladies and Lords of the summer
You have shown the most
Remarkable of all virtues
For today as you sit
Wrapped in earned robes,
Literally or figuratively,
I see you filled with courage.
For although you might all
Be bright, intellectually astute,
You have had to use courage
To arrive at this moment.
You may be,

As you are often described,
Privileged, which of course means
Wealthy, or you have been born into an ongoing struggle with
    need.
In either case, you have had to develop
An outstanding courage to
Invent this moment.

Of all your attributes, youth,
Beauty, wit, kindness, mercy,
Courage is your greatest
Achievement,

For you, without it, can practice no other
Virtue with consistency.

And now that you have shown
That you are capable of manufacturing
That most wondrous virtue,

You must be asking yourselves,

What you will do with it.
Be assured that question
Is in the minds of your
Elders, your parents, and strangers
Who do not know your names,
Your fellow students who
Next year, or in the years to come
Will sit, robed and capped
Where you sit today,
And will ask the question
What will you do?
There is an African adage

Which fits your situation.

It is, "The trouble for the
Thief is not how to steal the Chief's
Bugle, but where to play it."

Are you prepared to work
To make this country, our country
More than it is today?

For that is the job to be done.
That is the reason you have
Worked hard, your sacrifices
Of energy and time,
The monies of your parents
Or of government have been paid
So that you can transform your
Country and your world.

Look beyond your tasseled caps
And you will see injustice.
At the end of your fingertips
You will find cruelties,
Irrational hate, bedrock sorrow
And terrifying loneliness.
There is your work.

Make a difference
Use this degree which you
Have earned to increase
Virtue in your world.

Your people, all people,
Are hoping that you are
The ones to do so.

The order is large,
The need immense.
But you can take heart.
For you know that you

Have already shown courage.
And keep in mind
One person, with good purpose,
can, constitute the majority.
Since life is our most precious gift
And since it is given to us to live but once,
Let us so live that we will not regret
Years of uselessness and inertia

You will be surprised that in time
The days of single-minded research
And the nights of crippling, cramming
Will be forgotten.

You will be surprised that these years of
Sleepless nights and months of uneasy
Days will be rolled into
An altering event called the
"Good old days." And you will not
Be able to visit them even with an invitation
Since that is so you must face your presence.
You are prepared
Go out and transform your world

Welcome to your graduation.
Congratulations

Poetry

To fling my arms wide
In the face of the sun,
Dance! Whirl! Whirl!
Til the quick day is done.
Rest at pale evening . . .
A tall, slim tree . . .
Night coming tenderly
Black like me.

(published in *The Collected Poems of Langston Hughes,*
Alfred A. Knopf & Vintage Press)

If African and many African American poets have one theme it most assuredly is "Wouldn't everyone like to be . . . Black Like Me?" Black poets revel in their color, plunging pink-palmed black hands deep into blackness and ceremonially painting themselves with the substance of their ancestry.

There is a flourish of pride in works which must stupefy

the European reader. How can exaltation be wrenched from degradation? How can ecstasy be pulled out of the imprisonment of brutality? What can society's rejects find inside themselves to esteem?

Aimé Césaire, speaking of the African, wrote:

Those who invented neither gunpowder nor compass
Those who never knew how to conquer steam or
electricity
Those who explore neither seas nor sky
But those without whom the earth would not be
earth. . . .
My negritude is not a stone, its deafness hurled
against
The clamor of the day;
My negritude is not a speck of dead water on the
earth's dead eye,
My negritude is neither tower nor cathedral. . . .
It perforates opaque dejection with its upright
patience.

(published in *Return to My Native Land*, Bloodaxe Books)

Césaire was writing in the same spirit as that which inspired the black American poet Melvin B. Tolson when he wrote:

None in the Land can say
To us black men Today:
You dupe the poor with rags-to-riches tales,
And leave the workers empty dinner pails.
None in the Land can say

To us black men Today:
You send flame gutting tanks,
Like swarms of flies
And pump a hell from dynamiting skies.
You fill machine-gunned towns with rotting dead—
A No Man's Land where children cry for bread.

(published in *The Negro Caravan,* Citadel Press)

Mari Evans gave heart to African Americans in general and women in particular in her poem "I Am a Black Woman":

I
am a black woman
tall as a cypress
strong
beyond all definition still
defying place
and time
and circumstance
    assailed
      impervious
        indestructible
Look
  on me and be
renewed

(published in *I Am a Black Woman,* William Morrow & Co.)

The negritude poets' exposition of oppression, in fact, was inspired earlier by the Harlem Renaissance writers. The American black poets heralded their blackness, carrying their color like banners into the white literary world. When

Langston Hughes' poem "I've Known Rivers" became the rallying cry for black Americans to take pride in their color, the reverberations of that attitude reached the Africans in the then French and British colonies.

Sterling A. Brown's "Strong Men" must have had a salutary effect on the African poets:

> *They Stole you from Homeland*
> *They brought you in shackles*
> *They sold you*
> *They scourged you*
> *They branded you*
> *They made your women breeders*
> *They swelled your numbers with bastards.*
>
> *You sang, 'Keep a inching along like a po inch worm'*
> *You sang, 'Walk together children . . . don't you get weary'*
>
> *The strong men keep coming on*
> *The strong men get stronger.*
>
> (published in *The Negro Caravan,* Citadel Press)

That poem, and Claude McKay's "White Houses" and Countee Cullen's "Heritage," were guiding lights to the colonized African poets. The Africans in the Caribbean and on the African continent had much in common with their black American counterparts. They had the onerous task of writing, in the colonial language, poetry that opposed colonialism. That is to say, they had to take the artillery of the foe to diminish the power of the foe. They meant to go farther; they hoped to, with eloquence and passion, win the foe to their side.

The hope still lives. It can be heard in Langston Hughes's poem "I, Too, Sing America."

I, too, sing America.

I am the darker brother.
They send me to eat in the kitchen
When company comes,
But I laugh,
And eat well,
And grow strong.

Tomorrow,
I'll be at the table
When company comes.
Nobody'll dare
Say to me,
"Eat in the kitchen,"
Then.

Besides,
They'll see how beautiful I am
And be ashamed—
I, too, am America.

(published in *The Collected Poems of Langston Hughes,*
Alfred A. Knopf & Vintage Press)

27

Mt. Zion

Once in San Francisco I became a sophisticate and an acting agnostic. It wasn't that I had stopped believing in God; it's just that God didn't seem to be around the neighborhoods I frequented. And then a voice teacher introduced me to *Lessons in Truth,* published by the Unity School of Practical Christianity.

Frederick Wilkerson, the voice teacher, numbered opera singers, nightclub singers, recording artists, and cabaret entertainers among his students. Once a month he invited all of us to gather and read from *Lessons in Truth.*

At one reading, the other students, who were all white, the teacher, and I sat in a circle. Mr. Wilkerson asked me to read a section, which ended with the words "God loves me." I read the piece and closed the book. The teacher said, "Read it again." I pointedly opened the book, and a bit sarcastically read, "God loves me." Mr. Wilkerson said, "Again." I wondered if I was being set up to be laughed at by the professional, older, all-white company? After about the seventh repetition I became nervous and thought that there might be a little truth in the statement. There was a possibility that God really did love me, me Maya Angelou. I suddenly began to cry at the gravity and grandeur of it all. I knew that if God loved me, then I could do wonderful things, I could try great things, learn anything, achieve anything. For what could stand against me, since one person, with God, constitutes the majority?

That knowledge humbles me today, melts my bones, closes my ears, and makes my teeth rock loosely in my gums. And it also liberates me. I am a big bird winging over high mountains, down into serene valleys. I am ripples of waves on silver seas. I'm a spring leaf trembling in anticipation of full growth.

Gratefully I am a member in good standing of Mt. Zion Baptist Church in Winston-Salem, North Carolina. I am under watch care at Metropolitan Baptist Church in Washington, D.C., and I am a present member of Glide Memorial Methodist Church in San Francisco, California.

In all the institutions I try to be present and accountable for all I do and leave undone. I know that eventually I shall have to be present and accountable in the presence of God. I do not wish to be found wanting.

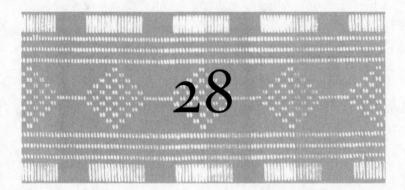

28

Keep the Faith

Many things continue to amaze me, even well into my seventh decade. I'm startled or at least taken aback when people walk up to me and without being questioned inform me that they are Christians. My first response is the question "Already?"

It seems to me that becoming a Christian is a lifelong endeavor. I believe that is also true for one wanting to become a Buddhist, or a Muslim, a Jew, Jainist, or a Taoist. The persons striving to live their religious beliefs know that the idyllic condition cannot be arrived at and held on to eternally. It is in the search itself that one finds the ecstasy.

The Depression, which was difficult for everyone to survive, was especially so for a single black woman in the Southern states tending her crippled adult son and raising two small grandchildren.

One of my earliest memories of my grandmother, who was called "Mamma," is a glimpse of that tall, cinnamon-colored woman with a deep, soft voice, standing thousands of feet up in the air with nothing visible beneath her.

Whenever she confronted a challenge, Mamma would clasp her hands behind her back, look up as if she could will herself into the heavens, and draw herself up to her full six-foot height. She would tell her family in particular, and the world in general, "I don't know how to find the things we need, but I will step out on the word of God. I am trying to be a Christian and I will just step out on the word of God." Immediately I could see her flung into space, moons at her feet and stars at her head, comets swirling around her shoulders. Naturally, since she was over six feet tall, and stood out on the word of God, she was a giant in heaven. It wasn't difficult for me to see Mamma as powerful, because she had the word of God beneath her feet.

Thinking of my grandmother years later, I wrote a gospel song that has been sung rousingly by The Mississippi Mass choir.

> "You said to lean on your arm
> And I am leaning
> You said to trust in your love
> And I am trusting
> You said to call on your name
> And I am calling
> I'm stepping out on your word."

Whenever I began to question whether God exists, I looked up to the sky and surely there, right there, between the sun and moon, stands my grandmother, singing a long meter hymn, a song somewhere between a moan and a lullaby and I know faith is the evidence of things unseen.

And all I have to do is continue trying to be a Christian.

PHOTO: © BRIAN LANKER

MAYA ANGELOU was raised in Stamps, Arkansas. In addition to her bestselling autobiographies, including *I Know Why the Caged Bird Sings* and *The Heart of a Woman,* she wrote numerous volumes of poetry, among them *Phenomenal Woman, And Still I Rise, On the Pulse of Morning,* and *Mother.* Maya Angelou died in 2014.

ABOUT THE TYPE

This book was set in Requiem, a typeface designed by the Hoefler Type Foundry. It is a typeface inspired by inscriptional capitals in Ludovico Vicentino degli Arrighi's 1523 writing manual, *Il modo de temperare le penne*. An original lowercase, a set of figures, and an italic in the "chancery" style that Arrighi helped popularize were created to make this adaptation of a classical design into a complete font family.